T0209277

A Poet's Journey

Faith Humor Reflections

RICHARD A. CARDNER

WESTBOW
PRESS®
A DIVISION OF THOMAS NELSON
& ZONDERVAN

WestBow Press books may be ordered through booksellers or by contacting:

WestBow Press
A Division of Thomas Nelson & Zondervan
1663 Liberty Drive
Bloomington, IN 47403
www.westbowpress.com
1 (866) 928-1240

ISBN: 978-1-9736-5488-9 (sc)
ISBN: 978-1-9736-5487-2 (hc)
ISBN: 978-1-9736-5489-6 (e)

Library of Congress Control Number: 2019902157

Print information available on the last page.

WestBow Press rev. date: 03/13/2019

I wrote these poems over a period of years and have collected them here. The dates are when I wrote or revised them.

I give thanks to my family, especially my wife, Linda, for support. The Poetry Email Workshop of the Poetry Society of New Hampshire has been of immense help, and its members put up with my puns while commenting on many of the writings. In line with this, some of the poems may mention the prompt. This refers to the workshop's prompts for its members for a given two-week period. Other poetry critique groups in Arizona, New Hampshire and on-line have added their voices. Of course, the writings are my responsibility, and for this I am sure both my family and the groups are grateful.

My ideas have changed as I have grown, and I assume that ideas and methods used in earlier poems would be changed were I to address the topics today. I especially hope that I have not offended my Creator or mislead His creatures or children.

Richard Cardner
February 2019

Contents

After

After the star,
after the birth,
after the shepherds
and angelic mirth,

after the manger,
after the magi,
then life's not seen
with an earthly eye.

December 28, 2007

Ages

When I was ten,
I thought growing older meant driving a car—
and it did.

When I was twenty,
I thought growing older meant marrying my star—
and it did.

When I was thirty,
I thought growing older meant raising our kids—
and it did.

When I was forty,
I thought growing older meant being on the skids—
and it did.

When I was fifty,
I thought growing older meant I'd be retired—
and it did.

When I was sixty,
I thought growing older meant in aches I'd mire—
and it did.

Now that I am seventy,
I think growing older means growing closer to God—
and with His help, it is.

December 13, 2012

Amish Parents

(After the slaughter of their children)

The oaks knew
their acorns were crushed
and sprouts snapped off.
Oh, they knew
as only parents can know.
The oaks grew
by living water,
wept,
grew to forgive
the slaughterer;
thus, oaks grow.

October 14, 2006

Asunder

With a tip of the hat to Peterson's translation of James 2:19–20

The CSI people
were called in
to ascertain
what had been.

After hours of painstaking,
tough review,
they published their
thoughtful purview.

"This was once one man
in whom life's blood
worked with his faith
in doing good.

But a deceiving liar,
we surmise,
taught him with
deception's disguise

so that the man
who once was one
split faith and works
and now is done."

February 27, 2009

Belief

With a tip of the hat to C. S. Lewis

Above the trees,
the sun rises.
I see it, and
by it, I see.

The shadows shrink
below the trees;
I believe. It's
the sun, I think.

Within the boughs,
the green leaves turn
to their light—to
spread, grow, live, bow.

Under the bark,
the sap rises
to feed those leaves
that hide the lark.

It all fits now:
the shadows recede,
the leaves turn;
the sap, the bough

are from the sun,
the source of life.
But I must ask,
whence comes the sun?

October 19, 2011

Brown's Junction

Ruby enjoyed the banter with strangers.
"Are you happy here?" the customer was asking.
Ruby responded, "Sure, why not?"
already in her task, basking.

"It is so far out of the way,"
replied the tall saleswoman.
"Town seems dead,
with everything banned."

She delivered the meal
and pulled up a chair
when the redhead
invited her with care.

"Wouldn't you like to experience the world?"

"Yes, and I do, you see."
"How so?" was the world's weary reply.
"Here, the world comes to me,"
said Ruby with a twinkle in her eye.

February 2, 2014

The Candle

The candle's light was oh so brief
but lit our path with love's glow
that stayed the evil of the night.

We clearly saw the world's dark road
and torrent's watery grave below.
The candle's light was oh so brief.

We feared lest terror's winds would snuff
the taper's blaze from candle flows
that stayed the evil of the night.

We slipped, we fell, and we forgot
what we learned when candle showed
(the candle's light was oh so brief):

the love, the blessings of our God;
the strength to stay the course bestowed
that stayed the evil of the night.

The candle's gone but lights the sky
where it went with God on high.
The candle's light was oh so brief
but stayed the evil of the night.

The candle's gone but lights the sky
where 'twent with God on high.
The candlelight was oh so brief
but stayed the evil of the night.

February 9, 2019

The Christmas Candy Cane

A story of old,
or so I am told,

of a baker's reasons
to love the season.

White for purity,
like the new snow.

Red for sacrifice,
the gift you know.

A shepherd's hook
resting in the stall;

a *J* for Jesus,
who saves us all.

December 14, 2010

Choices

Written when I had trouble writing about an
assigned prompt for my review team

Why, oh why
did I
choose fall
for the theme?

It's too worn,
too warm
to freeze
thought—yet, team,

here I stand,
no words
in hand
for my peers.

I'll send this.
Please hiss
it not.
It is sincere.

September 27, 2005

Choose One

It
was a dark and stormy night.

It
was
a dark and stormy night.

It was
a
dark and stormy night.

It was a
dark
and stormy night.

It was a dark
and
stormy night.

It was a dark and
stormy
night.

It was a dark and stormy
night.

September 3, 2009

A Christmas Poem for My Grandchildren

The pond is frozen;
the snow's in the air.
The worms are resting
in their underground lair.

The thermometer's low;
the ice is slick.
But Christmas is near,
and, I hope, Saint Nick.

I have not been as good
in all I do.
(Not as good as I should
have been … and you?)

But I know
on Christmas morn,
God's gift of forgiveness
was certainly born.

So in all the hustle
of this blessed season
and all of the bustle,
let's see the real reason:

a little babe born
in an animal manger
so no one need be
to God's love a stranger.

And to my grandchildren,
wherever you are:
know that I love you,
whether near or far.

Christmas Season 2010

Christmas to Remember

The cold air,
breathed,
tingles the nose
to a knowing of winter.

The snow crunches
as we walk to church
and alerts us to snowman snow
we can use tomorrow.

The friends gathered
raise our energy
and awaken the old tunes
of the faith and love.

And Santa, poor Santa,
tries to unite two worlds:
he gives the gift of giving
to a world of glittering greed.

December 24, 2011

Deborah

Based on Judges 4–5

She was the judge of Israel.
Beneath the Deborah Palm,
she held court for people's resort,
providing Hebrew calm.

The people of that ancient land
did evil in God's sight,
so by Sisera they're cruelly held
with chariots of might.

"Barak," she said, "is God's own choice"
to beat the king cruel
and seek to better Israel
without the foreign rule.

"I'll go," said Barak, "but not alone.
You must with me come."
"Done," she said, "but understand
there's no glory for you, son."

Barak charged down Tabor's slope
and beat the enemy band.
Sisera ran to save his skin
but died by a woman's hand.

March 28, 2009

The Decision

I walk down the street
in a windy, cindery city.
I see her ahead
near the library,
her layers of coats and shopping cart
clear signs of her place.

Old questions arise:
Give money to be drunk away?
Pay a misty, swirling mind?
Donate to an old prostitute?
Subsidize a con?

I am close to the clearing
shoppers made by
avoiding her spot.

I am getting close
to the clearing of ideas:
mercy, or justice?

Those thoughts fill my mind
as my warmly gloved hands clench.
I hunch my shoulders

and avert my eyes
to think more clearly.
As if not seeing would help me think.

Her voice pierces the veil
of my retreating, hurrying hood,
but not my mind-shielded heart

as I drive one more nail.

December 2005

Dropped

I wish I could walk like they do:
to move, to hop, to run.
They smile at those times.

I wish I could fly like they do:
to soar, to glide, to reach for the sun.
They trill at those times.

I wish I could swim like they do:
to dive, to float, to flip with fun.
They rejoice at those times.

I cannot do those things.
I am rooted here,
where my acorn dropped.

March 12, 2012

Echoes

If only I had heard,
"Come follow me."

I wish I'd eyes to view.
"Come, you will see."

I didn't know how
to think of Lazarus.

When I found out
good comes from Nazareth,
whatever happens now
is past last breath.

November 30, 2007

Eden Remembered

Decades decimate my body,
dragging it into December.
Decades decorate my soul
with Eden remembered.

December 8, 2008

Evergreen

I drove onto the tidy ground
and saw the clear, bright stones.
I found the family's resting place
as hallowed eve's moon shone.

A grand sire here, there an aunt,
cousins too far to count.
I am wary, lest I'm dragged down
with baggage they had brought.

I'm told we'll meet across the road,
no tears, no grief to bear.
That will be the miracle;
let's pray we make it there.

January 2006

Everything

Using the line "Everything desirable is here already in abundance,"
from Linda Gregg's "A Dark Thing Inside the Day," for inspiration

Everything is here:
that desirable food,
the right temperature,
companionship.
Everything is table-set to sate our needs
here in this complete garden.

Yet already we seek more and,
in this want-wallow, we do not see the
abundance that dances in reach.

August 23, 2011

Fireflies

The moon, rising in the east on a cloudless night,
spread fireflies on the sea water's waves.
The children, backs to that scene, stretched their necks to see
and count their change, whining about their lack of wealth.

December 6, 2010

Free

Freed dove,
three times seeking,
futile flying two times.
Love looking to light, land, live—
love freeing dove.

June 22, 2006

The Gathering

I went to our gathering,
a family affair.
I liked the laughter that was
near, not far.

Then one of my cousins said,
"It's my time to leave,"
but spent a happy, boisterous hour
taking that leave.

Next, an aunt with but one child
smiled goodbye, left shyly,
quietly, quickly, lightly,
with not one sigh.

When my turn comes 'round
with family gathered here,
will it be one goodbye or many,
with gladness or fear?

November 7, 2007

43

Gift

Sun
rise.
Treetops
alit with
gold, warming the green,
slowly op'ning my morning gift.

June 11, 2006

Grass

———•———

Wind tore the mountain;
fire ate its way unhindered.
Grass grows green anew.

July 20, 2008

The Gray Day

A mixed-gray layering of clouds
covers the earth.

Not the white fluff
of a cumulus

nor the towering, noisy
thunder boomer.

The clouds sit there
above, quiet, cold.

Night dawns slowly
with no rosy glow,

just the slow slip
of gray into slate.

In the morning, we wonder
at the thermometer;

is it broken?
The temperature still

the same as last evening
and a death-dealing frost

averted by our cold,
gray, heat-reflecting friends.

September 12, 2010

Here I Am

Father,
our Creator:
all-knowing, sustaining,
powerful love, hallowed spirit,
awesome.

Contrite,
I wait for You.
Incomplete without You,
sinful in soul and action, I
await.

Thankful
to talk with You,
to drop my pain and rest,
fearful I'll think or do amiss.
Keep me.

I'm here
asking for help
to do what will please You,
bring You glory, honor and praise.
I wait.

February 9, 2017

Hurried

I
am
not
Hurried.

I
am
not
Harried.

I am
not worried.
I am not scared.

Insendingthispoemout.

June 15, 2011

I Knew

I remember you
with your two-year-old shrieks,
your first-grade reading,
your youth baseball.
I'm so thankful.

I remember you
with your good GPA,
your basketball play,
your scheduled life.
I'm so thankful.

I remember you
with your class service,
your spreading laughter,
your fine art skills.
I'm so thankful.

I remember you.
Did you think I'd forget?
I knew you'd come
to visit my grave,
and I'm so thankful.

May 23, 2006

Irk Some

"A stitch in time saves nine,"
is what my mother taught.
So react promptly
was a household ought.

They say, "Haste makes waste."
Mother taught it too.
So wait to answer.

Now what do I do?

March 18, 2007

Javelinas

The javelinas
trooped, tromped, chomped. Silly girl thought
it was her garden.

April 27 2010

Job Number One

I walked down the street
from my home,
past the one-engine
fire barn to Charlie's store.

I offered my services,
and he set me to work
stocking the shelves,
mostly lower shelves.

I must not have done too well, sadly.

He let me go
in a few minutes
after paying me
with an ice cream sandwich.

I ate my wages.

I didn't work there again,
but I still talk with him
as we walk among relatives' graves
sixty-five years later.

He still has that impish
smile and elfish Irish wit
with which he can make you enjoy it
when he puts you down.

Well, maybe I didn't do too badly.

March 28, 2010

Labor

The combine crept through
golden, grain-filled fields.
My grandfather called,
"Catch up and help!"

My six-year-old legs
labored and ran toward the
weathered, outstretched hand
that hauled me up.

No rest.

Breathing dust,
holding burlap bags,
dripping sweat,
wiping brow.

Noon rest.

Savoring bread
I had not baked.

Drinking water
I had not drawn.

Resting in shade
I had not grown.

Receiving love
I had not earned.

September 5, 2006

Lakes

Among the hills is a lake:
fresh, fish full, and clear,
filled by springs,
fueling fun.

Its fullness flows out, sounding
down rocks, falls into bogs, then
wets fertile fields,
slowly filling

a desert lake in the cliffs:
foul, dread, full, and thick.
Filled by love,
it leaks out none.

February 12, 2007

The Last Word

Last is a small word,
but it means a lot.
Here are some readings
you can pick up fast.

It can be the end,
most recent,
authoritative,
or up-to-date.

As a unit of weight,
80 bushels,
640 gallons, or
2 tons of goo.

It sits at our feet
like a human foot.
We mend on a last
or shape a shoe.

It continues in time
or in force.
It's the most recent stock traded
in a time past.

It is not deep,
this effort of mine.
Thus ends this little poem
at long last.

October 31, 2005

Lean

The bare tree leans from the woods;
its water-soaked roots lifted, drip.

February 6, 2012

Looking

I had this assignment, you see,
to people watch
and then write a poem
concluding … hmm … something.

So I sat in the mall
at the food court
(A court? Is it a sports arena?),
knowing it would have crowds.

It went like this.

A man munched on a Big Mac,
looking … around.

Then there were the tweens:
stylish, as they understand style,
looking at hunks and chatting
self-consciously while sneaking
glances at those deemed worthy.

A tired woman
pushes a child in a perambulator
(There, that dates me.)
and looks quickly, not daring, I suppose,
a direct look at strangers.

A man.
Some teens.
A woman.

All
looking and
listening.

Hmm.

I have it:

They must be
writing a poem.

November 8, 2008

Looking Eastward

I am sent by the elders
to the big waters
by the sun's rise.
To report on huge canoes
with cloth above and many water poles.

I see men
in their camp,
men with red and yellow hair,
and beyond them was their
big canoe.

At the men's sides
are long, shiny things
that cut so cleanly,
like arrows only bigger.
There are animals easily pulling big baskets,
rolling along on round things.

My report filled with good will be.

And in the east
beyond the canoe
is a cloud
gathering other clouds.

Not like our western clouds
that bring
the three sisters' rain,

but slowly growing,
darkening,
filling the sky
with lightning,
like men's unsheathed, side-hung arrows.

Wind moves the water,
like their animals the baskets,
easily moving it.

The men turn, smile, and kneel
before the wave-breaking,
pine-splitting, dune-moving storm.

My report ill will be.

May 10, 2006

Marriage

They came from opposite sides
across the dunes,
with their
cotton-filled mouths,
sand-abraded,
blistered skin.

Each riding on their own wave,
oasis seen
with its
quenching water,
soothing aloe,
shading palms.

In storm they saw each other,
mirage melting,
but marriage melded.

With their
thirst slacked,
skin smoothed,
they rest in shade.

January 21, 2006

May I?

"May I talk at you?"
"Well … umm … uh."

"May I talk to you?"
"Hmm o … kay."

"May I talk with you?"

"I would love it!"

May 13, 2008

Mirror

What do you see
in that mirror—
in that ego-fogged,
dull, world-pitted glass?

The outline of the handsome Adonis—
a flawless specimen?

Riiight.

Here, let me turn up the light.
And now what do you see?

The beer belly,
the pocked skin,
the dull eyes
and yellow caried teeth—those that are left?

Wrong again.

For when the light
that casts no shadows comes,
you will see as you are seen,
at that time,
by the only thing that matters
and not a reflection of matter.

Will you be spotless or not?
You choose.
And, oh, please don't be wrong the third time.

July 16, 2011

The Narrows

Who owns the narrows runs the bay,
as ships require a home.
The cable exec has the say.

The media needs that way
to propagate its tome
Who owns the narrows runs the bay.

We think knowledge we can sway,
and falsehoods out we comb.
(The cable exec has the say.)

That our brains are just for play;
our knowledge's so much foam.
Who owns the narrows runs the bay.

In minutiae mired, we stay
struggling in muddy loam.
The cable exec has the say.

The answer to this play
(For this poem, it's the sum):
Who owns the narrows runs the bay.
The cable exec has the say.

November 21, 2005

Nicodemus

Based on the story of Nicodemus, found in the
Gospel of John 3. Quotes are imagined.

Nicodemus's Secret Journey

I walked a path, wond'ring if the man
had done the miracles and is the One.
My council'd stop me if it knew my plan,
but still I must know—is he the Son?

Jesus and Nicodemus

"Rebirth gives you the kingdom's key—believe it !"

"How so? To enter twice their mother's womb?"

"Flesh gives birth to flesh," but Spirit to Spirit.
So I "must be lifted up"; belief ends gloom.

The Council Decides

The council said the credulous mob's cursed;
this movement must be crushed, so kill its head.
My hope beat back my fear—"Condemn Him first,
but do not hear Him? Is our own law so read?"

Hope

We took Him from the cross—placed Him in the tomb.
By Sunday's dawn He's gone, but hope is given room.

November 14, 2015

October

Don't wonder at my tomb
nor burden self with hate;
you think to weave life's fate
on God's eternal loom.

Don't ponder at my grave
nor long wait and hedge;
you too are near the edge
despite your face made brave.

You laugh or are somber,
but know this, earthbound friend:
the pattern's near its end.
It's already October.

October 6, 2009

An Old Line

There he was,
born on third base,
thinking he had
hit a triple.

August 14, 2010

On Thin Ice

Your quick response
and poem to rate
is appreciated;
'tis its fate.

Here's my answer
so's not to be late.
But I'm running out of "cutesy";
please don't berate.

I like the words
in their rhyming state,
and sounds repeating
one could not hate.

The eight repeats
nicely therein,
so I'll stop now
as the ice is thin.

October 1, 2008

Padanaram

The children came across the field.
First through foot-tall grass, then lawn,
laughing, skipping, running, smiling.
Back from their swing with the hammock,
telling tales of their hammock spills:
new learnings from new leanings.

Summer 2009

Palms Up

Sunday:
mob's cloaks and palms
making smooth the Lord's way.
Friday: mob's death cry, "Crucify."

Silence.

Sabbath's
silence, then third
day: quiet, empty tomb!
Body stolen? Who dared believe
risen?

Not foes
nor all fast friends
nor we with history
to lead forth our Thomas-like minds
from things

to truth
that something big
happened that day. So big
that futile men killed as though love's
a thing.

April 6, 2009

Poet's Progress

The itsy-bitsy poet
went on the quatrain way.
Down came the critics
who thought they had some say.

Out came work's spirit,
which dried up all the tears,
and the itsy-bitsy poet
wrote quatrains many years.

January 24, 2011

Punishment

I think I have seen this title somewhere but do not recall where

A professor told me,
"Puns are the worst form of humor."
This worsted dressed man also
pitched the idea that "There could be no left-handed catchers."

This caught me in left field, a fresh man freshman;
doubtlessly I was full of doubts.
I did not find punishment in puns,
nor see why his way of catching was better.

I wager that a bettor would bet on any
catcher who handles pitches well,
and I do not need to run home
to base my opinions.

October 30, 2009

Quickly

Written at a grandchild's request

I cannot write a good poem
in just a single minute.
It takes some thought and work
I have to put in it.

"Please write a poem now."
My grandchild asked the favor,
so I've done the best I can,
but it won't have much flavor.

January 23, 2011

Remainders

The spring garden's
soil smells
so sweet when fresh
and warmed by longer days,

is fresh from
winter's ice and sleet,
from death's grip,
to feed us anew.

Gripes about death
shrivel and shrink
as plastic wrap in a fire,
while life and love remain.

August 27, 2009

Return to School

An old story

"Micky, time to get up.
It's the first day of school,"
Mother called up the stairs.
No answer came—not cool.

She went up the stairway
to ensure his waking.
She looked in the room;
she saw the blankets quaking.

She sat there by her son,
giving his hair a muss.
"Son, you should get up now—
not maybe, it's a must."

"I can't go to school, Ma.
There are three reasons why
I have to stay right here,"
he told her with pained cry.

"The teachers laugh at me.
The kids bully and tease.
The janitor shoves me
though I say, 'No, please!'"

"I know your dilemma,"
she answered with no guile.
"There are reasons to go,
though it seems the last mile.

It's important to learn,
and gym is fun. Most of all:
you need to go, and soon,
'cause you're the principal."

September 9, 2011

Rhoda

The idea for this is from Acts 12

That night I was seized by toughs
in Herod's bloody game.
Sixteen soldiers were assigned
to guard my weakened frame.

Two thugs I slept between that night,
in chains of iron bound.
When then the light shone in my cell,
my ribs they roughly found.

"Quick, get up!" the vision said.
My wrists now were free.
"Dress and cloak yourself," he said,
"and quickly follow me."

I went with him out of that place,
past guards and guards again,
till at last the Antonia gate
opened on its own.

In the length of one short street,
I found myself alone.
I had no doubt an angel of God
freed me from a tomb.

I went to Mary's house straight away,
where they prayed I'd be freed.
My knocks at the outer gate
only a slave did heed.

Rhoda recognized my voice
and ran to tell the crew,
"Peter's at the outer door.
God has been with you!"

"You're out of your mind," they said,
but she knew what she knew.
They prattled, "Not Peter,
but a vision's fooling you."

"We're busy praying deeply, deeply
to deliver Peter now.
Go back to your duties, slave,
and bother us no more."

But I kept knocking, knuckles red;
at last they opened up the door.
Their doubts had stopped their ears
to answered prayer, Rhoda and more.

October 16, 2007

Rock Wreck

The water drips
on granite's face
in wind; ice's freeze
splits rock apace.

The sun-melt ice
feeds grass's seeds,
whose roots wreak rock
with gentle plead.

March 29, 2006

Salt

───•───

You are the salt of the earth. (Matthew 5:13)

YOU are the salt.
Keep your saltiness
or be out by default.

You *ARE* the salt,
or be out by default
and be called less.

You are the *SALT.*
Maintain your saltiness.

July 8, 2008

School's Out

School is hard for me.
They always want much more.
Their reasons I don't see,
like what's the square of four.

So, I am always sent
to the room so immense,
where the huge principal vents
at my stammered, dense defense.

Slides are meant to be
full of laughing kids and glee,
but all the teachers laugh at me
as I often skin my knee.

So when June's around,
I run and am free.
I chose to be a teacher—
how'd that come to be?

June 23, 2009

The Short Line

A tip of the hat to the song "Where's the Line to See Jesus?"

I walk down the mall's hall.
There's quiet music so loud
I can hear the words,
but not the meaning.

There are displays so bright,
they shut out the light,
demeaning the season.

Why am I here?

Oh, yeah. To get a gift.

Let's see ... gold
to gild our granite hearts?

Frankincense
so we smell better,
or better yet don't smell?

Myrrh.
For death rites?
For a baby?
Foreshadowing?

I walk by
Victoria's (not so) Secret,
collusion in our confusion
of lust with love

I preview diamonds.
You'd think they should be red
for all the blood shed over them.

It is time
to go.

As I leave,
I pass a long line waiting for Santa.
I wonder, "Where is the real Christmas?"
as I avert my eyes from
a beggar softly singing,
"Where's the Line to See Jesus?"

December 23 2010

A Sleep

A tercet triplet

I usually enjoy the day.
The meals, the friends, the work, the play
fulfill my life in every way.

I go to sleep without a qualm,
but then I find my mind uncalm.
It has no more of Gilead's balm

until I'm blessed with honeyed thought:
to read the Word that God has wrought.
Then sleep returns just as it ought.

August 7, 2015

A Solid Learner

She learned slowly,
building her skills by repeating
sights, sounds,
smells, touch, and taste.
Slowly she learned.

She learned slowly;
she saw brothers,
heard Handel,
smelled incense,
touched talc,
tasted toast.
Slowly she learned.

She learned, ever so slowly;
she saw poverty others missed,
heard harmony in the universe,
smelled refuse,
touched the untouchables,
tasted the tasteless.
Slowly, ever so slowly, she learned.

And when her time came,
she knew
love,
and heard the
"Well done"
said lovingly, steadily, slowly.

February 6, 2009

117

Speed

At times I read the Word with speed,
to get it done before my work.
And when I do that way read,
I miss so much and lose the way.

At times I read the Word with speed
Because I've read all this before,
"I know this stuff." No words I heed.
I quickly pass to seek world's ore.

At times I read the Word with care,
unrushed by mind's unending pace,
and see the life inside the Word
and marvel at unbounded grace.

March 13, 2011

Sunblock

———•———

When we block the sun,
no wonder we're affright
to see what remains
after we've stopped the light.

February 9, 2006

Sweet

My tongue lies.

Sugar is good
in its eyes, and
bitter is bad, but
that meds belie.

July 26, 2007

Thanklessness

Luke 17:11–19 NIV

We were there in that hut,
nine of us, and one of … them,
with nowhere to go.

Condemned by rotting flesh
that kept us here with no friends,
with nowhere to go.

We heard of a healer
coming to the area
with somewhere to go.

He must pass the cabin;
the crowd told us he was near.
We shouted, "Heal us!"

He looked straight into us,
saw us for what we were, and said,
"Go to your doctors."

With scar-marked faces down,
we shuffled away, but …
the disease dissolved.

You cannot know our joy
as we went running our way;
all but … him, the alien.

He went back to the man,
grabbed him by his garment's hem.
"Thank you for the cure."

"Were there not more, alien?
Were not nine with you cured?
You alone returned?

I see you have been cured;
deeply faith cured now;
you have somewhere to go."

November 29, 2011

There's No Point to Geometry

With a tip of my hat to a child who first presented this idea to me.

There's no point to geometry.
We use triangles to prove.
But triangles are made of lines,
lines made of points.
Points don't exist, so
lines don't exist.
Then triangles don't exist, so
there's no point to geometry.

September 24, 2010

Yoda Rethought

"Do or do not, there is no try!"
outburst Yoda to Walker of sky.
Overstatement is sports-like thought,
but should we seek to make it an ought?
To try has hope that lets us fly.

September 23, 2009

Printed in the United States
By Bookmasters